Luna Park

Grevel Lindop was born in Liverpool, educated at Oxford and now lives in Manchester, where he is a freelance writer. His books include *A Literary Guide to the Lake District*; *The Opium-Eater: A Life of Thomas De Quincey*; *Travels on the Dance Floor*; and *Charles Williams: The Third Inkling*, as well as editions of Chatterton, De Quincey and Robert Graves's *The White Goddess*. *Luna Park* is his seventh volume of poems.

Also by Grevel Lindop

Poetry

Against the Sea
Fools' Paradise
Tourists
A Prismatic Toy
Touching the Earth (Books I–IV)
Selected Poems
Playing With Fire

Prose

The Opium-Eater: A Life of Thomas De Quincey
The Path and the Palace: Reflections on the Nature of Poetry
A Literary Guide to the Lake District
Travels on the Dance Floor
Charles Williams: The Third Inkling

As Editor

British Poetry Since 1960 (with Michael Schmidt)
Thomas Chatterton: Selected Poems
Thomas De Quincey: Confessions and Other Writings
The Works of Thomas De Quincey
Robert Graves: The White Goddess
Graves and the Goddess (with Ian Firla)

GREVEL LINDOP

Luna Park

CARCANET

First published in Great Britain in 2015 by

Carcanet Press Limited
Alliance House
Cross Street
Manchester
M2 7AQ

www.carcanet.co.uk

We welcome your comments on our publications
Write to us at info@carcanet.co.uk

A CIP catalogue record for this book is available from the British Library

ISBN 978 1 857549 87 4
The publisher acknowledges financial assistance from Arts Council England

Typeset by XL Publishing Services, Exmouth
Printed and bound in England by SRP Ltd, Exeter

For Caroline, Helen and Lucy
who helped

Contents

I

II

III

IV

I

Cosmos

Between Orion and Gemini, an almost-full moon.
Wrinkled tidewater tilting at the lips of Morecambe Bay.

Galaxies of cow parsley edging the valley fields.
Slow explosions of lichen on the fellside boulders.

The long-armed yew gesticulating at your window:
ancient growth-rings cupping a still more ancient hollow.

Old glass: molten tremulous lungful of human breath
spun flat, cut to rippled squares, set in the dusty casement.

Grain of the living oak, stopped dead in your tabletop.
Cobweb at the table's corner a map of skewed co-ordinates.

Your table lamp fed by Heysham's uranium rods,
Haverigg's twinkling windfarm, buried cables along the Duddon Valley.

Your mobile: lit menu, notional time, no signal.
The mountain: against the black of the sky, a blacker black.

The labyrinth of your fingerprint: Chartres maze stretched to an oval.
The fieldpaths crisscrossing in the palm of your hand.

An ink-slick spreading in the pen's furrow:
gold keel ploughing an ocean of churned Norway spruce.

All of it drawn and drawn into the pupil's black hole,
the dark that cannot be seen, the space that is everything else.

The Maldon Hawk

he let him þa of handon leofne fleogan
hafoc wið þæs holtes, and to þære hilde stop

– 'The Battle of Maldon', AD 991

And so, dismissed, I rose on a wingbeat
over horses already scattering to the wood,
unwanted as men turned to their war.
Vassal set loose from his master's service,
blameless outlaw freed to the houseless wild,
circling, I watched thickets of metal and leather
crowd the shallows of the deepening tide.
Now as I scour the air my heart divides
between longing for a man's call and the wideness of the world
where I got honour by my endgame, pleasing nobles
in the hour when the bright dove fled the man-flung hawk.
I pivot at flight's apex but will not return,
though my jewelled eye sees each ring on his corselet
catch sun as he merges into the mass,
death-besotted warriors on their way to darkness.
Gladly I would stoop a last time into his language
but already battle's whirlpool sucks him in, his face downward,
nameless and eyeless among the iron helmets.
I am a word forgotten from his story.
He is a landmark fading from my sight.
Men had seemed to have some special knowledge:
now the sea-wind tastes of death, they rush towards it –
whether to sing with saints or feast with battle-fellows
or lie at a tree's root until the world ends
they know no better than I. Never again,
child of the waste moor and the tufted woodland,
will I perch on that wrist, grasp the bone beneath.

Bed

It's a great book. Open the covers,
soft and floppy as the hide of a giant folio,
patched and stitched. Inside are the stories
of our thousand and one nights, the radiant
conceptions of our children, dreams and memories
neither time nor water will wash out
nor the wringing of hands.
Written in those sheets are tears, arguments
with the absurd logic of marriage, the justifications
of ageing, and over them the crushed
roses of what we hoped for, still fragrant
when you turn the cover or fall asleep reading
late at night.

And it's a boat,
wooden raft that tilts on the tides of sleep
riding the diurnal hurricanes
of light and dark that sweep across the planet
changing the shape of our room,
the moon dragging trees' fingers and clouds' hair
like colossal seaweed and shadowed shoals
over our tumbled bodies. No craft has sailed
on stranger voyages,
not the hollow ship of Odysseus when he woke
to find himself Sinbad. In its square hold
we've travelled out of our world
to talk with the dead, make love to strangers,
remember how to fly.

Also (forgive me, love)
it's a grave, the narrow space where each day's laid
to rest in almost peace,
where bodies, humped and shrouded, wrapped in cotton
or linen – those fibres briefly removed
from the earth they grew in – nightly await
the morning's provisional resurrection
that one day will not come: book, boat, grave, world
closed, floated, lost, vanished away

and us with them, into what other dream
who knows, into what other waking,
into what perhaps, into what other love?

Pencil

Like texture, love a pencil –
almost weightless in the hand,
tipped with that flecked cone of soft cedar:
the point at first hypodermic-sharp,
then an aircraft-nose, streamlined but soon
softening, snubbed by the flow of paper
that streams against it, an abrasive sky
whose friction will humble it to a mere nub,
unhelpful cobble trailing a blurred line or
scraping along on wooden uppers. And the fascination
of its so-called 'lead', that peculiar hue
a black not black, one of those troubling blacks
like marcasite or haematite:
almost a metal somehow, almost a paste.

Contrast the lacquered coat, slick as a new car's
cellulose, goldblocked with capital text
(9H, HB, BB) chunky enough to dint the spine
of a clothbound hardback. Then as you unreel it
slowly, through the sharpener, over the days,
a wood silkworm yielding a streamer long enough
to festoon this room all round. A spiral
staircase that unravels its own tower;
wooden Rapunzel nothing but her plait,
it dwindles at last to an irritating stump
fit only for the dolls' house, too dinky for human
paws, to be lost under the hall table or
magicked to wherever
used-up pencils go. And what does finishing
a pencil mean? It's an asymptote –
you never reach the end, only get closer
then a bit closer still. But for now,
go ahead, reach for the sharpener, you deserve
point, clarity, a pristine world
for your thoughts. Though there's imperceptibly
less of it each time, and a little less.

Pupil

Pupil: Latin *púpilla*, little girl, orphan.
To the Greeks, the *koré*, the young girl, the Persephone
snatched to the underworld. Lost child staring from the dark –

from the cave of the eye where Plato thought we sat,
bemused by coloured shadows. Plato, pupil of Socrates –
the face most often in his eye, most splayed on the convex mirror.

Or Ananda, the Buddha's pupil:
orphan poised on fathomless dark,
the black disc painted in last, animating the gold statue.

Female, like the soul: *anima*. Without
its diminutive, it becomes
pupa, a girl, a doll:

crisp mummy-case,
dead mother, Russian doll, chrysalis:
patterned shard twirling on silken

thread from a leaf-tip, or niched in dust
between two churchstones. Dormant
memory, about to split its seedhusk

and spread the vast flowering map of its veined wings:
psyche, the butterfly. Your face blossoming
from the past into my pupil, apple of my eye.

Round your own pupil, the Iris – Roman rainbow-goddess,
green, brown, hazel, watercolours of the forest-fringe,
circle of living barcode

machines will scan to number you at immigration
before you walk towards me, wide-eyed,
pupils shrinking from the light.

Pomegranate

Apple-red, streaked and speckled apple-gold:
poma granata, 'the grained apple', fruit
that's mined and faceted with grains of ruby.

Garnet, your favourite stone: Latin *granatum*,
from the pomegranate, whose seed it much resembles.
So the names coil round upon themselves.

Like a small bomb: grenade, Spanish *granada*,
a pomegranate. The fuse, the flower, has gone:
at the serrated neck a brown dry powder.

All Hallows' Eve tonight. I watch you slice
through the red ventricles, crushing out pink juice
to eat with chicken in the early dark.

Your knife blade bleared the colour of a winter
sunset, you discard the leathery membranes.
Feed me a few seeds from dripping fingers.

Suffolk

It's about the horizontal, a landscape
much like the lines of this poem,
one stratum above another, ruled
by sediment, weather, gravity, the plough
and light, which is this moment muddy and wet
so there's no clear boundary, the distance
not horizon but melt into more distance,
more white like an unwritten page, or cold pressed
rag awaiting watercolour. Remember
verse is *versa*, the turning of the plough
at the furrow's end: once Horace's white oxen,
now, in English, a solitary tractor, sugar beet,
and the train drawing another line, green and silver
between mud and ditches, between here and there,
a slow half minute between the black and the white.

Maryport

Pallets and cardboard are stacked for Guy Fawkes
on tussocky grass; in Strand Street, front doors
are ruby glass and white UPVC.
New pebbledash covers crumbled brickwork.
Plump lads in knitted caps and short wellies
('Y'all reet?') sit on plastic boxes to tie hooks
then cast from rods mended with gaffer tape,
and gulls squall fractious over the chunks
thrown by a man with an iPod plugging his ears
and a plastic bag of buns. At the harbour mouth
a Sunday sailor takes out a red sail,
a single fin on glassy water. Forget
the reprocessing plant. The Golden Lion, Lifeboat,
Middle Tap, Sailor's Return and Captain Nelson
are open. And here by the last house
a rusted anchor towers above us,
eroded by salt air: one giant fluke skyward
beautiful and obsolete as a whale's tail-
flick, and the other embedded in concrete.

Fortune: Nottingham Goose Fair, 1971

'Cross my palm with silver.' She really said it,
and in those days a fifty pence piece was worth something –
a new coin, mysteriously seven-sided,
certainly something more than half a pound –
though I'd chosen her because she didn't look
the part. No hooped gold earrings for her. Hair in curlers,
feet in bedroom slippers – not like the shawled and be-ringed
ladies outside the other vans that crowded
the sloping edge of the suburban field.
So I crossed it, and sat while she scrutinised mine
and murmured over it, a singsong recital
of the wonders that lay ahead. What do I remember
from her litany, that seemed not to pause for breath?
'You'll marry for thirty.' (What on earth did *that* mean?
Anyway, I wasn't going to.) 'You'll have three children.'
(Oh no I wouldn't.) 'What's your ambition?'
'To be a poet.' 'You will, but you've a lot to learn first.'
(I couldn't argue with that.) There was so much more,
but before I knew it my time was up,
it had all flowed through me. I couldn't grasp any of it:
so reassuring, so almost hypnotic that voice
still in my ears as I stumbled for the blind
confusion of the bead curtain and caravan steps,
when I touched grass I'd already forgotten my future.

Luna Park

Forget the Opera House, forget everything. What I remember
is Luna Park, unreachable behind
chain link fencing and KEEP OUT signs.
The ghost of a funfair, due for demolition –
a landscape of fantasies that would be
nowhere soon. I could see The Bug,
a giant ladybird, shiny scarlet
with black spots the size of car tyres;
The Clown, vast face coloured like an iced cake
with red nose and corrugated ruff.
No hint of what they did or how you rode them.
The top car of the Ferris wheel teetered
as if each moment about to go
over the top, though it was only the wind
that rode there. The roller-coaster's three cars were stuck
at the bottom of their downward graph.
I stared a long time through the wire. Then
followed the others away. A pale moon
rose over Bondi, whitening empty breakers. Lights came on
along the rocky shore but Luna Park just faded
into blackness until the moonlight
sketched in a few of those thin girders
exposed by fallen plywood. I still hankered
to find a gap in the fence. Here I am
ten years later, like a child with no money,
hopeful, face pressed to the steel mesh.

For Our Lady of Guadalupe

The taxi windscreen's broken,
lightning-starred with a crack from one corner:
signature of a stone from the Oaxaca road.
It drops me by the shanty-town of stalls
where I will buy her plastic image later –
garish, I hope, and cheap,
for kitsch is authenticity.

A jagged rift of space
splits the old basilica's perfect Baroque,
an intricately-cracked stone egg
atilt on sliding subsoil where the Aztec
city's lake was carelessly filled in.
Crowds pass its listing shell without a glance,
heading for the concrete-and-stained-glass

swirl that mimics
Juan Diego's cloak, where she appeared
and painted her own image on the fabric
to show sceptical bishops
how perfect love could visit a poor Indian
after the wars, and fill his cloak with roses.
Now the cloak's under glass behind the altar.

A priest celebrates Mass,
but we walk round the side
to queue for the moving pavement that will take us closer,
its mechanical glide into the dark
floating us past the sacred cloth
and her miraculous, soft, downcast gaze:
not Spanish and not Indian but both,

lovely *mestiza* Virgin, reconciler
who stands against the flashbulbs' irregular
pizzicato of exploding stars,
and while we slide on interlocking steel
opens for us her mantle, from which roses
pour and pour in torrents, like blood
from a wound that may never be healed.

The Letters

This must be where the alphabets come home to roost,
streaming at twilight like a fine black smoke
from every corner of Mexico: thicker and thicker
through the cooling air of the *Zócalo*,
along the shaded side of the cathedral, and in
under the arches of this stone colonnade,
to drop at last into the shallow wooden trays –
their many compartments like tiny pigeonholes –
into which a printer's expert thumb is flicking, even now,
the few sorts that fluttered, here and there, into a wrong box.

Soon after dawn one side of the square is lined
with housepainters, electricians, plumbers hoping for work.
They sit against the cathedral railings, each
with a hand-lettered cardboard sign affirming his profession.
Perhaps you'll read it while another man brushes your shoes
on an antique box with a brass footrest the shape
of a miniature footsole, gleaming like gold,
polished by all the larger soles that have trodden on it.
But behind you as the last tinny bangings die away
from the cathedral bells, and the sun starts to bake the pavement,
under the cool white arches the alphabets are sleeping.
They have borne so much, they have so much to forget.

Even for us it's hard not to be drawn in. Each square stone pillar
has its glassed frame full of competing samples
from an ordered world: wedding-invitations, christenings, condolences,
business-cards, comings-of-age, first communions
with sprays of silver blossom, angels, madonna lilies.
And over your shoulder, as you admire, you come to feel
the cavern of the little shop, cool as a catacomb,
where you could have your poems printed, or your menu,
or the announcement (with a black cross) that your father has died –
each given definition by a man with a black thumb,
spectacles high on his forehead, and a cherished machine
all black cast-iron and shining steel rollers, built
lifetimes ago in Stuttgart or Birmingham.

And empty in front of each shop are two folding chairs
and beside them a frail folding card table with a typewriter –
electronic, the old kind with a daisywheel
and shiny black plastic ribbon. And this is where you'll come,
if you can't write, to dictate your letter;
and if you can't read, to have your letter read
aloud, and over again, so you'll remember everything.

The Notes

Only notes from the journey;
here are five thousand pesos,
Colombian, *Banco della Républica*:
a bearded man and a fly with transparent wings,
an avenue of thin trees, and a frog –
all of it the lemonish, pallid green
of an evening sky. Turn it over,
and a young girl in a Victorian dress
wanders down between the spindly trees
towards a vast moon, past a shallow Greek dish
on a plinth with a long, long inscription
in tiny letters: even a magnifying lens –
the one I use for the dictionary – can't decipher it.
A quill pen (or is it an exotic curling leaf?)
floats at one side. Money is a dream,
it seems to say. *Art nouveau* decorations
sprawl and fiddle over the empty spaces;
a ghostly face appears as watermark
when you lift that moon to the light.
A thousand Bolívars,
Banco Central de Venezuela:
thin and fragile, yet almost leathery
with handling. Bolivar's longnosed, sensitive face –
and behind it a great book, laid open, full of writing:
Acta Solemna de Independencia…
En el nombre de Dios…
again quill pens, quill pens in a dish,
quill pens in inkwells; and the watermark
Bolivar's ghost, haunting an oval space.
On the reverse a great hall, men in high collars
queueing to sign a document at a table.
And there are the signatures, framed at the bottom:
tiny, curly, illegible to us as Arabic.
Most of it's burgundy
as if someone had spilled a glass of wine over the plate
and printed with it in a pinkish purple.

How solid the US dollar tries to be:
those swashbuckling metallic flourishes,
the word and the figure ONE all over the place
as if worried we might mistake it for two or three.
An eye in a shining pyramid:
'a new order of the centuries'. Is it giving light,
or watching us? The stonework's made substantial
with little cracks and chisel marks, but they're only
lines drawn on the paper, like the cross-hatching
inside the letters and round the borders,
and the signatures of Secretary and Treasurer. Writing, writing,
as if everything would come real if we could only write
hard enough, if we could only forget
money is everything we don't have.

The Key

This time the key comes down in a white sock –
small enough, it looks, for a child. Yesterday
it was a twist of paper, the day before
a spectacle-case, plastic. That's how you visit
in Havana. Expected, you squat –
hoping for shade – on a doorstep across the street
to squint up at the flaking elaborate
balconies – blistered shutters, washing, bicycles –
waiting for a familiar face to appear.

Or, coming unexpectedly, you stand
on the pavement to yell, and whistle shrilly
with two fingers if you can, until the same face
peers down at you. Then she'll disappear
to fetch the key, return to choose a gap
between infrequent cars, motorbikes, rickshaws,
and at the best moment toss it down
wrapped in something soft and conspicuous.

You run out like a cricketer to catch it
but never do, it skitters on the warm air,
pirouettes sideways. No, you will always
miss, it plunges to the dust while she leans
over to watch you pick it up and stroll
to the cracked, sun-pitted street door.

Turning the key
this moment, I step through and shut myself
in the cool musty dark by the electric
waterpump and the black serpent-coil
of cables writhing from the rusty fusebox.
I stand to breathe a moment, then start up
the twisting marble stairs, climb the five flights.
She will be waiting by the stairhead
to kiss – '*¿Como estás?*' – and take the key,
then slam and bolt the door, slip off her trainers,
choose a CD. Now we shall dance and dance.

Cigar

It would have, unrolled, a small book's
surface area. My first was a gift
from the man at the next table
of the pavement café at the Hotel Inglaterra.
He worked, he said,

at the Partagás factory, where they read
the newspaper aloud all morning,
and in the afternoon novels and poetry
while, adept as conjurers',
the workers' hands rip, stuff and wrap. More words
went into it than I shall ever draw out.

The tobacco-god is a bird with scarlet plumage
and mother-of-pearl eyes. His four
attendants are the green
spirit of the fresh leaf, the brown of the dried,
the red spirit of fire and the blue of smoke.

The red visits only for flaring instants;
is fickle, demands nurture. The green
is memory and imagination. The blue
is a girl dressed in feathers: lapis, lavender, sky.
When she kisses

her tongue is sharp as sea brine, chocolate, chilli.
She says the word *tabaco* is Carib,
from a language whose last speaker
has been dead four hundred years. But the brown

lives in my hand this moment, brittle
and crisp as a chrysalis. Filtered
through his crushed spirals,
molecular poems thread themselves
into my genes, become part of the air I breathe,
the words I speak. Both of us end in ash.

Cuba Café

Mo's café has a bicycle hanging from the roof,
also white roses, a child's scooter, cabin trunks
and a Dansette portable record player. Guitars,
books, a rifle, old 78s and racks of wine
up there are perfectly normal,
as are the plastic palms and the great sweeping
ceiling fans that sail over your head while you admire
photographs of Castro, Marilyn Monroe, Charlie Parker
and the Ratpack, or watch the grainy videos
of Tito Puente on one of the six TV screens
among the strings of flashing lights and the shadows in the mirrors,
finishing your Sol or Corona. And here's Mo,
with his gold earring and towel, beginning another
supercharged salsa class (keep up or you go to the wall),
glistening with heat from the dance, the old pipework
and the rough brick. Drawn up on the pavement
is his classic car: not a Dodge or Plymouth
but the 1956 Vauxhall Cresta he calls *Lo-*
lita, her paintwork all gleaming burgundy and grey,
polished to such a mirror sheen that when you step
out into the Manchester weather, just the sight of her
(in the gold light from the café)'s enough to make you smile.

Lilacs

After so many years, the white lilac
this spring blooms purple as well, mauve cones
chequering the white. A bird-sown volunteer,
or grafted stock at last shooting up, distinct?
A richness given by time, anyhow,
the doubled colours a wall of fragile vision
before it all turns brown and adds to the summer
dust. And my children, now in their twenties,
each the unforeseen, unforeseeable;
and grandchildren, each unimagined in all the worlds
that went before. Let me give thanks to time,
savagely-masked Cronos who eats his own children,
but also the virgin mother who gives unblemished
things we dreamed of, and the dreams themselves.
Odd-one-out of the eleven dimensions,
not to be measured or agreed on,
weightless water where each swims at his own pace
even as the current speeds to the waterfall's lip.
Where did you catch me up, time, in your eddy?
On what bank will you lodge me, in what sea
lose, erode, dissolve not just my bones
but each molecule, atom, particle, vibration?
No end to your invisible labyrinth,
your measureless windings, at once our freedom
and our chain. Time, anyhow, to give thanks for the lilacs,
for the light darkening now over the garden.

In the Baptistery, Torcello

Again, it's the angels we enjoy
among the mosaics,

the Powers with their Roman steel
bonnets and slender spears,

Principalities with elegant lozenge-
shaped shoes tied at the instep;

those that balance small flames
on their hands, or the pretty

bodiless Seraphs who are only
child faces in a whirling ruff of wings.

They take no part in the story,
are not prefects

opening gates for the blessed who troop in
bound for Abraham's bosom,

nor do they sweat in the boiler-room
like those devils busy

forking the damned as fuel
into a bestial mouth.

They are serene as music,
come to us from another world

or a different religion.
They understand more and are more:

their gentle gold eyes acknowledge us, admit
that they too are only visitors

to this turbulent, moralistic,
saints-and-sinners cosmos:

halo'd with perfect circles, not
troubling their heads about it.

Silver

I

There was no money for engagement rings,
or almost none. No gold, no diamonds.
We found a shop that had Tibetan silver
and bought each other rings. The moon and stars:
for you a clouded white moonstone; for me
a star sapphire like a drop of midnight sky.
They didn't last: the metal was too soft, the spiral ends
of mine caught one day on a drystone wall –
or was it a barbed wire fence I was climbing?
Somehow it vanished. But by then we had
gold wedding rings and the sun had taken charge.
Still those rings expressed an equation.
The moon can fall from the sky, the galaxies
implode. But in the place
those rings told of, nothing was going to change.

II

On a path beside the River Allen,
as we walked back after a day's riding,
what was it called our attention
through the summer dusk across the glints
of swirling water and its silver eddies?
Among the long grass and the cow-parsley,
intently watching us: a hare,
bolt-upright, ears pricked, standing to attention.
We stared back:
stopped, still, hardly breathing, our eyes on his
for how long? Two minutes? Three? Until he
gathered himself and leapt, hung in the air one moment
curved like a question-mark
and vanished into long grass, deepening twilight.

III

Too many moons to fill an almanack:
the half, the quarters and the slices between
black new and silvercoin full –
the pearl tossed and netted in webs of cloud,
the thread of light with the dull disc in its loop,
gold shaving afloat on the horizon of harvest –
How many times did you call me from the house,
or from my desk to the window, simply to see?
Should I string them all on a necklace for you?
Impossible, though you gave them all to me.
Still some of their light reflects from memory.
Here it is, distant gleam on the page of a book.

IV

Reaching, one afternoon, the end of the wood
we paused under silver birches and heard
at the edge of hearing a light pattering –
was it or wasn't it? Then saw the air
was full of something dustlike, something falling
softer than dew, covering, softly covering
us: tiny, primrose-yellow stars,
the flower, or was it pollen, of the birch?
We stood and let it happen:
sometimes you simply recognise a blessing.

V

Your broken arm: elegant in the x-ray
as if designed by Charles Rennie Mackintosh –
the delicate fluting of the radius,
forming, with the ulna, an *art nouveau* lancet
lovely as cathedral tracery
or angled stems of an exotic plant,
on the silver-grey of the x-ray plate:
ghostly, subtle, the tracing of an inner
structure to your body; the small fracture
hardly visible. I'd always known
you were beautiful. Here was confirmation:
even after death the archaeologist
might say it, fifteen hundred years from now:
Yes, look at her, she was beautiful.

VI

The image softens and returns
more than you gave, if only
because not everything's clear:
the oldest mirror is the best
so long as just a trace of silvering
remains. We soften into time,
a stranger kind of looking back,
love in the bloom that speaks of loss
not yet but richer for its loss.

The House under the Crag

The drive straggles to farm track: two broad ruts,
a strip of grass and camomile between.
Old blue BMW pulled in on the slope
by the drystone wall. We leave our car
alongside and walk up to the house.
A hanging gutter-end; upper windows
blind with cataract of dust and web.
Flaking paintwork. A kerfuffle of dogs
scrabbling and barking from a metal trailer
by the barn. We go round to the back.
Stone steps, blistered woodwork. A brown door
wide open. Beyond, a sepia kitchen:
Aga, worn rugs, cluttered table. Then, at my left,
as if carved into the high backed chair,
a man's pale face: staring blue eye, arched eyebrow,
wisps of white hair. Hands spread, fingers
apart on the stained shirt, his
mouth opening, silent. I try 'Good afternoon?'
Indecisive movements: mouth, one finger.
(Stroke?) 'We wondered would you mind if we
left our car there, by the other one? A couple of hours?'
—'Eh, you'll need to ask *him*.' One finger flaps,
gesturing vaguely over the shoulder. 'You'll
need to ask me brother.' We exchange glances;
hesitantly turn to the other room.
            Dressing-table; enamel pot
in brown tubular frame; drawn faded curtains
filtering light the colour of Lucozade.
And on the double bed, diagonal, knees bent,
stiff as if newly dead, a man.
Asleep? Grey trousers, tweed jacket, brown shoes.
'It seems a pity to wake him. The car'll
be all right, won't it?' —'Nay, he's boss.
Ask him! Ask him!' The finger flaps urgently.
We turn back. Cough gently. As if a switch
were pressed, the figure cants instantly vertical,
bolt upright on the bed. The same blue eyes,
yellowed skin, startled brows. 'Good afternoon,

sorry to disturb you, we just wondered
could we leave our car outside a couple of hours?'
'I'm a bit hard of hearing.' I repeat:
'...by the other one? Just outside your yard?'
'Aye. Aye.' Expressionless. 'Thank you!' He hinges
sideways again, inert, stiff, angular,
across the bed. 'Thank you so much.' – a grunt
or murmur, inarticulate, as if
already falling once more into sleep.
We back out. 'Your brother says it's fine.'
The flat blue eye watches us. The spread fingers move
uneasily. 'Thanks so much. Cheerio.'
And from behind us, faintly, with an audible effort
as we go down the steps, 'Cheerio.'
The dogs go berserk in their metal container.
The blue BMW has gone.

Man and Fox

A man in red on a green field walks.
Staring from the wood's edge, a fox.

Close to the earth, by his cunning
this man now has trapped the vixen:

with a knife slit her throat,
ripped off her red coat.

How hungrily then Reynard ate
the bloody flesh of his mate!

I watched in horror and pity
those cruel acts. How could such things be?

Departing at length from the green meadow,
close at heel like his own shadow –

fox to man now familiar,
obedient and bound. It can no other.

The Alder

Living in time, I would be
like the double-natured alder tree
that lifts new catkins and old cones
to tremble differently and at once
in the light and cold air of February.

II

Shugborough Eclogues

Spring

(i)

A scrying-stone there on the desk:
pale marble veined with rust and blood
picked from the earth at Cannock Chase
last spring. You take it in your hand;
the chill draws warmth out from your palm.
Flesh-coloured, heavy, hard, and cracked,
quartz-facets glinting faintly here
and here; an egg from which to hatch
imagination's clotted speech.

In spring we walk by Seven Springs,
fresh water welling from the earth,
a long pool welcoming the dogs
and children shrieking their delight;
the shattered water's upturned sky.

Another sky beyond them spreads
in clouds of bluebells on the slopes,
and there again metal and blood,
the copper drifts of oakleaves dried
since autumn on the sandy steeps;
the bracken and the bumble bees.
Then the shut mines, the concrete slabs
stopping the mouth of shafts that led
to coal and copper underground:
their stories lost beneath the pelt
of bracken, oak and birch and ling.

Along the ridge a cuckoo drifts
among the pines and comes to rest
slate-grey, unwieldy, ill-at-ease,
to drop his notes into blue air
between long silences. At last,
spooked by our outline, slides away.

The park wall cuts the forest. Cars
grumble across the cattle-grids.
We speak an ordered language here,
the past is now and knows its place.

(ii)

This is the gem you cut, Thomas Anson,
from emerald forest and sheer water
lightflooded on a still spring day like diamond,
a white house rounded like a cabochon
curved to its shadowed setting, and a garden
that melts to woods and fields, a truce
with wilderness. Arcadia has no time
but its own season, spring –
when all things are possible.
And this was your Arcadia: a phrase
from some Greek poet, Theocritus perhaps
with his 'full threshing-floor' and 'canopy
of green leaves'; Virgil's line about 'cold springs,
woodlands and soft meadows' –
words like a seed-crystal dropped
into the saturate solution
that was your mind, blend of philosophy,
ideal politics and peace.
Good farming, a republic
of shepherds and their friends,
temples half-hidden in the forest groves,
Reason in awe of Nature's majesty –
a tranquil Zodiac overarching farms
lamplit at evening, lullaby'd by sheep,
and watched all night by the observant stars.

(iii)

Disordered times: an almost rainless spring,
hot April, sun and freezing winds that bring
leaves and white blossom drifting to the door,
dusty and littered on this marble floor
too early in the year. What have we done?
Dry autumn's here when spring has just begun.
To walk these rooms and fields I drove today
down sixty miles of crowded motorway,
time-conscious, and contributing my share
of greenhouse gases to the patient air.
Was Pascal right, the source of all our doom
reluctance to stay quietly in a room?
Probably. Though the whim of weather may
this afternoon sweep all our doubts away
with pouring rain or April showers. Again
we settle for our time's peculiar pain,
our pride in knowledge, what we have to show:
still ignorant, we think we *ought* to know.

(iv)

In the dry gorge at Tixall, cut
below the bridge's parapet
over the hot neglected slopes
full of dead leaves and violets,
the words HÎC VER PERPETUUM:
'Here is perpetual spring' – recalled
from Bacon's essay, or those lines
in Virgil's *Georgics*, offering
'eternal spring, summer in months
not hers'. A promise or a threat?
Summer in spring. Disordered times.

In shade, we dream of Cannock Chase,
the wilderness outside within
the ancient wilds of Staffordshire
the Green Knight in the gritstone gorge

the green man sharpening his blade
the cries of children on the air
the virgin goddess in the wood
the maiden with her triple face
howling Diana Tervagans
avenging, still unsatisfied,
the tears that nourish Seven Springs,
the lifetimes still unreconciled,
Christine, Diana, Margaret
the shattered beauty in the leaves
faces reflected in the pool
the twilight of the darkening springs.

Summer

THE CAT ON THE MONUMENT

(i)

Dreams of summer, glimpsed
through portholes of green rain
as wind blows clouds and drifts of water
over the garden. He watches the Great Yew,
hugest in Britain and Ireland, the Tower of the Winds,
Demosthenes' Lanthorn shaking in the blast
like the cracked masts of a three-decker rounding the Horn.
Having his sea-legs
like any cat Kouli-Khan
could keep his balance but rather
resting in lazy stone prefers
to consider, reclined, these hurried impatient humans.

While pressed men died of scurvy,
Chelsea pensioners, their skins turned black,
teeth buckling in swollen gums,
he skittered below deck
outwitting rats in the long gallery
of steerage and chain-locker;
or in Peru tightroped a mooring cable
to vanish into the woods, returning
with a wriggling lizard or squalling shrew.
Then meticulous cleaning of whiskers, before
hopping daintily to the Admiral's table –
a china dish of white bread and sealmeat scraps
to enjoy, while mutinous hands below
fasted on brackish water,
on biscuit powdered by weevils.
To climb the shrouds in sunshine and fair weather
his delight. Not for him to be ordered aloft
in a freezing gale, when storms had shredded the canvas,
with sailors whose bodies alone could catch the wind
to give the vessel steerage-way past rocks.
Not for him, cautious, delicate-footed, to fall

from the rigging, like that castaway who swam so strongly behind the ship
he could never reach, whelmed at last as his friends
watched, helpless, throwing a rope, a cask,
only to prolong the inevitable drowning.

(ii)

In pauses of the rain, cities explode.
Walls of glass are shattered. Fire takes hold.
The things we want so much we come to hate
their absence and their presence drive us mad –
a three nights' party. Bang and Olufsen
smashed open, and Miss Selfridge up in flames.
Money is debt, so now the central banks
pour in more zeroes to fill up the void;
and banks are built, as Maynard Keynes once said,
of marble and mahogany, to hide
the truth that there is nothing real within.
A generation hooked on shopping blames
shopping's dark side; dreams of a feral tribe
unparented, unschooled and unemployed.

(iii)

Kouli-Khan surveys mankind
from Peru to China. Predators
and prey. That Spanish galleon
had no chance under George Anson's guns –
her cannon spent, her decks on fire and strewn
'with carcasses, entrails and dismembered limbs'.
A nest of mice, prey to the English cat.
Silver, loot from America, snatched from Spain.
Then the refitting at Canton:
silver fishheads in plenty
for Kouli Khan,
while Anson and the mandarins
gesticulate and bow in mutual bafflement.

(A hundred years before the Opium Wars
will teach China a lesson in hard trade:
that nothing stands against a drug cartel.)
Then home to London, where Peruvian silver
proceeds in triumph through the cheering streets,
rides to the Tower for minting into coins.

(iv)

The tides are fickle. Admiral Anson dies,
the money flows to Thomas, and this house;
nourished on blood and gunpowder,
the soil grows generous. Here is the model farm,
the sunny spots of greenery
as Thomas Anson girdles round,
with walls and towers, his fertile ground:
the Chinese House, the Doric Temple;
sinuous rills and lakes,
and, on each wing, a pleasure dome –
thirty-five years before the poet dreams,
on Bengal opium, of another Khan,
our suave cat's almost-namesake. Kouli-Khan,
tranquillity personified, surveys
Arcadia restored. The National Trust
proffers Platonic England, where we all
are democratic nobles, our republic
governed by taste and learning, as we know
aristocrats and shepherds are the same.
And still it rains, and through our faded summer
the stone cat dreams green dreams, a monument
patiently gazing on a monument.

Autumn

(i)

Bottle-green summer goes, a message tossed
from the tilting deck of earth
as the sun rolls round to the Virgin:
golden Ceres reaped, raped, turned again
to Persephone as the stubble is burnt,
ploughed back to dark earth.

(ii)

Bushy oaks host long pools of shadow.
The year, like the great lime, is giving up:
dead branches jutting from the living tree.
Indian summer congeals to a rich essence
sticky as the ichor of these plums
that lie too thick to gather on the ground,
amber shadows where the insects float.
The mower with his yellow ear-protectors
guides his roaring four-wheeled Ransome –
smell of oil and cut grass in his wake.

Indian summer. In the walled garden
exhausted vines flourish their leaves,
shrivelled and wilted in surrender. Here and there
a globe, sun-yellow, lies on bare
earth like an abandoned football.
Late pumpkin flowers, sorry yellow rags,
hide under foliage.

A scarecrow crucified upon a post,
old cardigan and trousers stuffed and tied,
guarding a row of dull blue cabbages.

Somewhere within this sunshine is a darkness.
Your skull fills with the cool wine of autumn.

(iii)

Past the Great Yew the Shepherd's Monument,
unvisited, gathers long shades
where shepherds scrutinise the brief inscription,
carved stone within carved stone: Poussin reflected
in a stone mirror. Silent language:
ET IN ARCADIA EGO. We are stilled.
Too many questions. Who am I, who was I?
I too am in Arcadia and know
this dark place is the source of all its meaning.
The shadow shows the carving its relief.

O. U. O. S. V. A. V. V.

O you

(*O you who turn the wheel and look to windward...*)

This is the garden's secret door
the way we enter and we leave
by pathways we cannot conceive
this is the dark secret of the garden.

(iv)

...While the sun's
cannonball sinks through smoky cloud
earlier today, fractured shafts
of last light through the park trees turning
lawns to a late sundial. *Memento mori.*

Winter

Green fields white-combed with furrows of thin snow.
A pair of lapwings tumble in the air,
squeaking and creaking as they flip and fan.
Black-earth molehills erupting through the snow.
Trees are sepia stains on a white page.

At Tixall, glum putty-coloured sheep
stand solid on hard inedible ground
a crow pecks and patrols. A rattling caw –
answered at once from somewhere in the wood.
By Tixall church, snow blankets the graves.

A single bell-stroke clear on the half-hour.

And Tixall Hall bleak putty-coloured stone,
empty towers and vacant arch, the trees
on either side, cedar and sycamore
equally black against an off-white sky.
The air is sharp against your living face.

The path to the canal is scabbed with ice,
snow cut to chevrons by the tractor's tread.
The lock dull grey, a sheet of pitted glass:
ghost-bubbles, blebs of air trapped underneath.
Ducks pad and slip splayfooted, near a swan
confined to one clear pool beside the lockhouse.

White mist on the towpath thickening:
sharp woodsmoke sweet from a black narrowboat chimney,
oilcans and bicycles heaped on the roof,
no one in sight. These vessels named for dreams:
'Event Horizon', 'Voyager', 'Arkenstone'
fixed in the ice.

                    Ignore signs saying CLOSED
to cross the park, snow crunching underfoot.
Blinds down and shutters locked. A house can hibernate.
Clean the carpets. Plan corporate events.

Visits from DEFRA in its purple van.
Ladders and scaffold climbing the rear wall:
yellow high-vis jackets on a platform.
Metallic tapping sounds arriving late.

Around the formal garden, shrubs and urns
bundled in canvas, strapped like straitjackets:
shrouded for their own good against the cold.
A *putto* dances naked with a swan
amid a pool empty except for snow.

The Chinese house is red lacquer on white,
the curved roof loaded with subsiding snow.
A willow's tresses captive in the ice.

The Shepherd's Monument takes on new light:
white marble whiter than it ever was;
dark lichened shades sunk deeper into shadow.

In Tixall wood, long ropes of ivy scale
the bare and pole-like trees. On the horizon
Cannock Chase spreads out its blue-green drifts:
fir forest against the sky, with bands
of white mist blowing over. At our feet
winter's soft rubbish clutters round the roots,
wet moss, dead leaves and crystal clumps of snow;
and there, surprising green, a patch of snowdrops
then more and more, between the thinning trees,
towards the light. And overlooking them
the arch that leads from nowhere into nowhere:
snow-crusted parapet, the carved stone leaves
crusted with snow, and then the sharp incision –
Roman capitals, the circumflex
cut with a careful classicist's regard
for quantity and grammar, sanctioning
nature's wild truth: HÎC VER PERPETUUM.

(April 2011 – May 2012)

NOTES ON *SHUGBOROUGH ECLOGUES*

Spring

'Ver perpetuum' ('perpetual spring') occurs in Francis Bacon's essay 'Of Gardens'; there is a similar phrase in Virgil's *Georgics*. Thomas Anson enlarged and landscaped Shugborough in the 1760s. Scholars have identified the Green Knight's lair in *Sir Gawain and the Green Knight* as Lud's Church in the Staffordshire Peak District. Diana Tervagans ('Diana of the Three Ways') is the underworld aspect of the virgin forest goddess Diana; invoked at places where three roads or paths met, she was so fearsome that her title, mispronounced, became our word 'termagant'. Here this formidable gatekeeper to the underworld becomes, and laments, the three victims of the 'Cannock Chase murders' of 1966–67.

Summer

The 'Cat's Monument' at Shugborough commemorates Kouli Khan, the ship's cat who sailed round the world with George Anson on his 1740–44 voyage. George Anson was Thomas Anson's brother; prize money from the capture of a Spanish treasure-galleon on the voyage financed improvements at Shugborough. The 'castaway' fell from the rigging by accident, becoming the subject of William Cowper's poem 'The Castaway'. Riots and looting took place in several English cities during the writing of the poem. I cherish a heretical view that Anson's cat may have been named after Kubla-Khan, mentioned in Coleridge's poem. 'Platonic England' is from Geoffrey Hill, 'An Apology for the Revival of Christian Architecture in England'. The stone cat stares across at the Shepherd's Monument.

Autumn

The Shepherd's Monument has a stone bas-relief of Poussin's painting 'Et in Arcadia Ego', reversed. Beneath is the inscription 'O. U. O. S. V. A. V. V.'. The solution remains mysterious. The italicised line is from T.S. Eliot, *The Waste Land*, IV.

Winter

DEFRA is the Department for Environment, Food and Rural Affairs.

III

Aril

Dare you
taste it?
Exquisite
the scarlet:
candied, waxy
as lipstick,
as cherry.

Carefully, carefully
peel back the pink skin –
gluey, glutinous,
smearing pink jelly.
Try
to pry
stone from cup.

The needled tree shivers.
The red cup is sweet,
you have been told.
It sticks to your thumb.
Taste the fruit, taste it –
a reluctant faint sweetness.
Taste it, taste it.
You have been told.

Note: The fruit of the yew is not a berry but an aril. Only the hard seed at its centre is poisonous.

Epiphyte

Neatly growing in the rowan's
armpit; noticed only
when I sliced a branch off, pruning –
Herb Robert, delicate fanned lace
of spread leaves, fractal
to catch light: each green webs
angled to drink
from the sun's fountain; roots
bedded in tree detritus to which now
my blade adds
saffron-tinted sawdust, new
grist to that delicate mill, and I
wonder for a moment, my eye
caught, drinking the sight, trying
to imagine the distillation of those
pink flowers, those scarlet berries.

Browside

Squat against the fellside, dragonskin roof
scaly with slates, and the slates scaled with lichen.
It has cavities, stomachs, eyes. Inconstant tides
of air, humidity, time, breath and heat
flow through it. Its bowels are the byre, a fetid
gold cave of straw, mud and dung, trickling
a tang of urine, fermenting interior dark
warm as a low oven. And its skin
rocky mosaic, like the piecemeal shell
of caddis larva – fieldstones, split boulders, slabs
of slate compacted to a mineral hide
that glitters in rainwater.
Leaning and shifting
its comfort as the wind punishes
or relents, it flexes a black oak skeleton,
thorax of attics and stairwell. Valley trees
from half a mile away down by the river,
its beams creak and strain to lineal descendants
of gales that flexed and rooted them as saplings,
or rather to the same gales, which have coiled and eddied
round the world sleepless since such airs began.
Here those intricate branchings brace to ribs
of roof and floorboard, vaulting the hall's belly,
the gutsqueeze torsion of a stair. Books lining the passage
are fishlike flakes of fleshy soft tissue
incubating long lines of the world's DNA
in papery layers, a pulped living assemblage
of mildew, dust, humidity that bulks
membranes of walls, swelling and shrinking gently
with seasons, weather and the ruminant browsing
of humans who benevolently infest
these cavities, with lambs, calves, the car
and the mouse that scrabbles its own urgent occasions
somewhere behind my bed, as I too scrape
paper and pelting rain plucks the roof at my head
while I drift in a crow's-nest of murmurs, one mind tonight
of this house whose long purposes are unknown to me.

William Wordsworth, Jr.

Poor Willie, rarely allowed
the full name's dignity –
unlike his famous Dad.
Sobbing outside Father's study,
his Latin not good enough.
'Slow learner' perhaps;
dyslexic, quite possibly.
'What shall we do with Willie?'
perpetual refrain in the family.
No head for the Law;
business not quite respectable.
Handwriting awful, anyway.
Send him to sea? Unthinkable
(John, William's brother,
heroic hope of the family,
drowned off Portland Bill
in the *Earl of Abergavenny*.
Enough of tragedy!)
Make him a parson? But no,
John Jr. went *that* way.
So good gentle Willie
did his best; assisted
Father with his minuscule
government occupation:
became Distributor
(sorry, *Junior* Distributor)
of Stamps for Westmorland:
collecting shillings and pence
for the tags on legal documents.
Buried, of course, at Grasmere –
scion of the famous family.
Regular churchgoer,
after all; and surely God
or whatever stands in for God
will have been kind at the end.
We can't all be Laureates.
Somewhere the last must be first.

Stones

after epigrams of Posidippus, c. 310–240 BC

I

I am (should that be 'we are'?) the poems of Posidippus,
a diminished chorus. Once we were quite numerous,
now only nine and a few scattered phrases –
something about a cylinder, a torrent,
the Indian hydaspes; and a delicate—
delicate what? I, or we, forget.
After 1700 years, how good will *your* memory be?
Most of us are poems about stones:
an unpromising subject, you think,
although your jewellery and your finest buildings
are made from them, the largest and smallest things
about you; and at your worst moments
your heart may turn to stone. We survive,
indeed, because we were pressed to a heart,
or the void where a heart once was. Our Nile-reed paper
recycled, folded to make a mummy's breastplate,
holes cut in us for decoration. Whose heart did we soothe,
into whose emptiness sing? Did he or she sleep better
for having a pectoral cartonnage of stone poems
over that central darkness? Did our lines breathe
for him, for her, did our rhythms lend a heartbeat,
our images dreams? And was that heart light?
Lighter than the feather on the scales of Anubis?
Still we give thanks to the dead,
the one we shielded, the one who protected us,
whose beautiful crust sailed through the underworld
to your day, dead lover with poems at the throat,
songs from a heart of dust.

II

You have the stones at your fingertips:
your task to write a commentary,
to clear and polish the stones, set them in context
as a jeweller might set them in a network of gold:
twisting, plaiting, a crochet of hard threads, wires
to hold them in place, linking each to one other.
Precision work: nothing I could accomplish
within sight or even recollection of you. One glimpse
of your face and my ideas scattered,
dropped beads exploding over the floor,
thread utterly lost. Lady,
fond as you are of novelties,
put that thought into your glass of blazing ruby
at the banquet. Let it capture (at least for one moment) your
melting glance.

III

Your father's rough-cut amethyst,
the topaz ring you bought at that backstreet jeweller's:
the milky opal at your throat, dangerous gem.
How I longed to be a jewel on your finger,
on that hand I held once, the amethyst my excuse.
I kissed your neck as softly as that opal.
I longed to decorate your throat with pearls.

IV

Both of us confessed to being tactile;
she (she admitted) hardly even beyond
the Oral Stage. Once, she said,
unable to resist that taut, plump smoothness
she'd lost control and bitten
her baby daughter's arm, making her cry.

And I had worse to tell, or weirder:
one day, in a circle
of cypress trunks, entranced
by the warm redwood smell, the soft dry fuzz
of that stained, flaking wood, its texture
an alchemy of pencil-sharpenings
and deep-piled blotting paper, I too gave in
and licked the bark,
not once but many times,
athirst and dry-tongued with the dusty velvet.

So there. She raised the wine cup and she drank.
I concentrated
on the firm tenderness of her arm,
the satin bloom of her skin.
(And the stone? I write this in pencil:
graphite, softest stone,
sheathed in fragrant cypress.)

V

Not rock crystal: polyhydroxyethylmethacrylate,
plastic used for monthly contact lenses.
A hydrophilic polymer –
one that loves water. Even so,
you said you wept so much over that lover
your lenses became useless,
crusted with salt. After you washed them
they were no good. Vision pitted with sorrow.
Well, I hope he was happy
or proud at least
to know he broke your heart/your plans (your own correction),
set that torrent flowing from the frozen
crystal of your heart, melted the ice
just once. Or is it true
as somebody once told me
(a blinding revelation):
it's the hardest-hearted cry the most?

How Often

How often they come back to us in dreams,
the lost ones, the long gone,
and most especially our parents –
godlike once adored, godlike feared or hated,
givers of everything, it seemed;
who took themselves away one by one
whelmed in a complicated tide of events
before the sorting-out had even started.

We meet them on the stairs or in the bedroom
or in a strange and damaged countryside,
and full, still, of perplexed concern carried
intact from when we saw them
last, that no amount of talking
could disentangle. What can we say
after all this? It seems, each time
as I spiral helpless towards waking,
I hear my own voice stammer, in shame,
nothing of love or gratitude but only,
lamely, those words that cannot be unsaid:
I'm sorry, I'm so sorry, I thought you were dead.

The Graveyard Yew

A root to every mouth, the legends say:
and how long must it take, growing by night
(surely it grows by night?) needling its way,
drawn by that faint magnetic field,
the sleepless memory of the new dead –
to pry through elm and lead,
till some weak joint or tarnished fold will yield
and let the roothairs in to feed
on the rich knot those loosening jaws held tight?

A negative of infants in their cots,
thinned by the black teat sucking at each face –
so you imagine it; the features blots
of shadow blurred and discomposed
around the fingers of a black suede
glove, the digits splayed
to point where each short story has been closed
in earth mid-sentence, softly laid
aside with only this to mark the place.

No: the yew's flesh is white, mottled blood-red.
You might carve two chess-armies from one trunk,
the scarlet-marbled buttermilk that's spread
like bull's flesh, or the fat that laps
the human struggles of a stopped heart
no voltage will restart.
On dark and day its rings are fed, it traps
those opposites with patient art,
the branches shading where the roots are sunk.

Once as the chainsaw bit into an oak
it kicked, sparked, stalled. Within the grain,
notched by steel teeth, acrid with the smoke
of sap and friction, two headstones
were bedded, swallowed in the live tree.
Those slabs of masonry
with name and date had parted from their bones
two hundred years, at length to be
carved out again, and set to stand upright

a few more centuries. In echoing air
a church spills mourners onto grass. Through tears
some step finding their way uncertain where
a hope still strains a heart, a ring
still burns a finger to the bare bone.
The yew's dark monotone
spreads underneath the organ, offering
a certain comfort now you stand alone.
The church is younger by a thousand years.

Exorcism

Now I remember.
It was late November:
up in the gallery
of the old library,
books and papers stacked away,
I was finished for the day.
All afternoon long
not once had the clang
of the metal gate to the stair
struck upon my ear.
Yet when I passed the last bay
the corner of my eye
glimpsed – surely – someone bent
over the desk, intent
on a book.
I stopped. Stepped back.
No one.
I shrugged, walked on.
Then, in July,
an exhibition, a party.
'What is this book-cathedral like
as a place of work?'
I asked a group of staff.
A general laugh;
predictable answers from most.
One murmured '…except for the ghost' –
gesturing at the last bay
up in the gallery.
Alert now, I pressed
and soon heard the rest:
the trainee in the stack
who felt eyes on her back;
talk among the porters
of someone who loiters
just out of sight
beyond the stairs at night;
slammed doors after hours;
cold air; shivers.

Unquiet spirit,
if you read this poem or hear it,
look up and know,
now, your time to go.
No longer search double columns
in calf-bound volumes
of incunabula
to fill the *tabula*
rasa of your soul.
Cease now: be whole.
Let all the long past
whisper to rest.
Let the uncertain future
become an empty mirror.
Go now: have peace unbroken,
clear as the unspoken
silence; perfect as the white space
after this
poem
is.

Shortest Day

Winter. Time to dig deep,
to fathom underground rivers of sleep:
follow the bleed of colours that spill
from the wounded side of the hill.
Time to interrogate time:
to measure nothing; to resort to rhyme.
Time to be thankfully lost.
Time to forget the cost.
Snow is too definite:
mud and mist come by night,
day is guttering of rain
disconsolate on window pane.
Time to read black books,
attend to backward looks –
the road reversed in the mirror.
Your life was human error,
the way down and the way up
like the inside and outside of a cup:
the same and different.
Time to follow the scent.
You know more than you think.
Become silence. Sink.

The Apple Pip

Small as an apple pip, they say,
my daughter's baby sleeps and dreams
and from the wool of sleep now draws
the new thread of a thin-spun life,
from clouds that catch among the stars,
from ripples in the blood's dark streams,
from breath and rain, from north and south.

I wooed my love with apples once
and now love plants another root
and unexpected pulls the quiet
around that tiny knot of life,
the seed that grows a labyrinth,
the child within the girl who lies
curled in her bed within the room
within the house, within the house.

Autobiography

After so long the shepherd becomes like the sheep,
the forester like the tree. My hand is curved
to the pen; my fingers' ends
will not now flatten to the laptop keyboard.
I was born in these sheets, my heartbeat
semicolon, fullstop; iamb,
trochee. My ribcage a sonnet.
My blood is ink now, that alchemy
that darkens as it transmutes, the whole life
distilled to letters like a swarm of bees
or beetles: sweet if you like to risk
braving their nest, or a pest that swallows
the waking world only to trouble our sleep.
You won't find me now: what there was
is pressed flat, a dry garden on the pages.
Bury me, and it will be between the lines.

Dictionary

After me, who will inherit these
two slab volumes
heavy as a breezeblocks, with the lens in its drawer
to capture streaming print like a child's net
dipped in a rockpool, or an entomologist's
flicked purposefully above a seething meadow?

All those pages: map of a labyrinth
and the labyrinth's self,
pollen trapped in earth, seeds in a tomb,
strings in hyperspace waiting to generate
worlds upon worlds upon worlds.
So many beautiful distractions!

Let it be wanted, if only as a doorstop,
this kingdom of a million secret doors
with other doors beyond them; or if only
for children to stand on to reach books from a shelf –
if there are still books; or if not, to reach a jug
or a jar – if jugs, jars, children exist

after so much has been thrown away.
Once I too stood on it,
to look out of a window and see a country
at which even now I stand and gaze
in a surprise that expands and still expands
until I can only say I'm lost for words.

Unknown Reader

He will be young and restless,
and some afternoon
will skim the poems to see if anyone
has felt that way before. He hasn't read
Dante or Baudelaire, but will one day.
Meanwhile he browses, almost wishing he
had never met her, it's all so intense,
but knowing he can never again step back
out of this bigger, older, bitterer world,
when he discovers an oracle in the pages –
like the shadow on a sundial never before
lit into three dimensions. He will read
about your dark hair, the mischief in your eyes,
your breasts the colour of rose quartz.
He will try to imagine you, and he will fail.

Oxford, Again

The stair is spiral, and its final turn
brings me a landing and a room
under the eaves, as white and small
as that of forty years ago –
the same blank folded space to colour in
with books and cards and sleep and all.

Gunmetal grey, heavy as lead,
the laptop eases to the desk;
and books fill out a shelf
barely to the mid-point, a verse line
several syllables short. Two are unread;
two others blank: those I must fill myself.

Outside, the masons work like Jude the Obscure
replenishing the college's stone leaves,
lions and saints. Rounding the quad
I met two men in blue coaxing a trolley
loaded with carious gargoyles and a thing
like a half-melted harp, the odd

wing lopped from an angel. Stacked on pallets
stood the new blocks of stone:
crisp, uncut, colour of grainy white
honey. The signs are good:
ash and red-berried rowan crowd the window,
over the bed a high uncurtained light

shows chimneys where two rooks at dawn
– the knowing birds of Cronos – hunch
to grate a few dark monosyllables
into the coming day. '*Cras*', they intone,
an omen that hides nothing,
more potent than the muffled college bells.

A pebble's throw away is Number Four
Broad Street, where Yeats once lived
and C.S. Lewis visited to hear
(fidgeting with uneasy fascination)
his talk of apparitions, magic, poetry.
Throw me another pebble, it lands near

the city's pivot, Carfax Tower. A third,
and there's the castle mound, newly unfenced
after a hundred years, for anyone
to walk upon and climb the grass
under whose pudding-basin mass
Merlin shut the quarrelsome dragons in,

one red, one white, whose bickering
disturbed the realm. Like two coiled springs they sleep
in tension, whilst their torque
empowers the kingdom. I set out the cards –
designs of Pamela Colman Smith,
her trips to London, Kingston, and New York

implying mixed-race ancestry as much
as her dark, sweet and round-faced smile: in this,
too, England's fitting prophetess. The querent
is crossed by Saturn, or the Hermit, Time,
lantern in hand; the Lovers overhead,
beneath his feet the Hierophant.

And this year sees my own Saturn return
a second, perhaps final time,
to where he stood when I was born. The sun enters the Virgin
today. Lines are drawn
through time and place, converging like a lens
so time is still. Still time. Time to begin.

IV

Hurricane Music

The grass verge in front of Fats Domino's house is strewn with splintered timber and black plastic rubbish sacks. But there's nothing wrong with the great man's residence, a modest yellow-and-white clapboard bungalow with 'FD' in cut-out wooden letters on the front rail. Mr Domino isn't at home, though his house – flooded when the levees failed – was repaired a couple of years back. It's the house next door that's receiving attention. A dozen teenagers in jeans, t-shirts and heavy gauntlets are hard at work, hauling out rotten floorboards, wielding brooms, cautiously hefting sections of cracked window glass to add to the growing pile of junk in the street. A curly-haired youth with ear protectors works his way along the narrow front lawn with a strimmer. Clouds of dust drift through the sunlit air.

A plump woman in blue overalls approaches to ask who I am. I introduce myself as a visitor from England, and she tells me her group, from an inner-city New York high school, has come to spend two weeks volunteering, clearing properties still derelict four years after Katrina.

The kids drift over, dragging off gloves, dust-masks bouncing around their necks. A skinny Puerto Rican boy shakes hands. 'How ya doin, man?' A solemn black girl with dreadlocks wants to know what the 'English government' would do if a city got washed out the way New Orleans did. Would they leave bodies on the street for ten days like they did here? Would they help people move back into their homes?

She gestures around. 'You'd think, like it happened four months ago, not four years.' She's right. Along the wide street every third or fourth house is boarded up, or just derelict: gaping window frames opening into darkness, sagging porches, front gates crudely wired shut, clapboard walls marked with the spray-painted hieroglyphs left by the police, the National Guard, the Humane Society: circles, crosses, numbers. (Is that four people found dead, or four animals rescued?).

'We just doing what we can to clear up, make this place ready for the builders to move in. Someone gonna come by later with a truck to carry away all this garbage. Ain't much we can do but we feel like we gotta do something.'

My host Ken, who's been hovering in the background,

introduces himself as a New Orleans resident. He adds that I'm a writer, and was recently in Cuba, writing about salsa. To my surprise this goes down well: there's a murmur of interest about Cuba, and a tall girl with tight curls and glasses, a plastic dust mask dangling from one elbow, says 'Cool! Hey, I always wanted to learn salsa.' I tell her if she can just go with the lead, I can teach her in two minutes.

'You can? Right now? Okay, yeah!' We step away from the piles of splintered wood and broken glass. She has a pair of red rubber builder's gloves flapping from the back pocket of her jeans. We partner up right there, on the dusty grass, and I count the beats while I show her the forward- and back-step. She's a natural: lithe and light-stepping, following my movements alertly. I take her into a turn and then risk finishing with a dip, flipping her gently backwards and lowering her until her head almost touches the grass before lifting her upright again. She squeals and bubbles with laughter as we step apart. 'Hey, that was *cool*!' She steps back, raising her palms to gives me a high five with both hands while the rest of the group applauds.

We say our goodbyes and they go back to work. As we stroll to the car Ken points at the house on the other side of Mr Domino's. There's a big coloured sign advertising a charitable foundation that claims to be 'Rebuilding New Orleans and its music'. 'That's typical', says Ken. 'Nice sign, but two doors away there's a house still derelict after four years. Not to mention the rest of the street.'

We drive further into the Ninth Ward, moving nearer to the canal whose levee broke on August 29 2005. Houses grow sparser – just the odd clapboard building here and there. We stop by a block of three houses, all empty and windowless. Two of them have jagged holes about three feet across in the roofs. Ken sees me staring up in puzzlement. 'People smashed their way out onto the roofs', he explains. 'The water forced them up into the lofts as it rose and they just had to tear their way out though the roof-tiles. Hopefully a boat or helicopter got them off alive.'

Each of the houses has two smaller holes in its brick foundations, one at either side of the front door, where looters have ripped out utility pipes to sell as scrap metal. We drive on again. Soon we're moving through a kind of flat savannah: fields or paddocks full of knee-high green plants, a fertile wasteland. I'm puzzled. Is this still the Ninth Ward?

'Lower Ninth.' Ken gestures around. 'This is where the houses used to be.' We roll slowly along a straight, narrow road. Every few yards another straight road opens up to right or left, and then disappears, masked by the greenery, as we pass on. I make an almost physical effort to get a mental grasp on what we're seeing. This grid of small concrete roads was the streets of a crowded neighbourhood. The green rectangles of lush grass and weeds were the city blocks. Everything – *everything* – has gone, and in just under four years wild plants have taken over the land.

'The floods just scraped everything away', Ken says. 'Pretty well anyone who was still in these houses was killed.' He stops the car and we get out. Apart from a faint simmer of buzzing insects, there's a large and very eerie silence. The land in front of us is flat and empty almost to the horizon. Ken turns and points. A few hundred yards behind us is a featureless grey wall maybe twice as high as me.

'That's the levee', he says. 'Behind that it's the canal, not the river, so the levee isn't banked up, it's just a concrete wall. You can have either an I-wall or a T-wall. A T-wall has a cross-section like an upside-down T, with the horizontal bar buried for extra strength. They only used I-walls here, so when the storm surge came and the level of the canal went way up, the wall just fell over. The entire tidal wave came pouring down here and swept everything away.'

We climb into the car again, out of the heat and the deafening silence, and cruise on. Here and there a buckled lamppost stands on a corner, still with a street name (Egania, Lizardi) on a metal plate pointing along a ghost street. We pass a couple of cleared building lots, and next to them several large, angular houses evidently in process of construction, though there's no one to be seen working on them. They have strange peaked roofs, solar panels, toylike powder-blue or buff walls. All are on stilts, though one has its rear end on the ground so it recalls a jacked-up, wheelless car. Jutting from the acres of green emptiness, the houses resemble weird, postmodern sculpture.

'Brad Pitt's project', says Ken. 'These are the houses being built by his Make It Right Foundation.'

'And who's going to live in them?' I ask.

'I don't know. A few very lucky people, chosen at random, I guess.'

Currently it's hard to imagine anyone managing to live in these odd houses, isolated in the midst of this green wilderness miles from public transport, shops or other people. Brad Pitt likes architecture, and these futuristic, environmentally-friendly, designer houses must have been fun to commission. They'd look good in Barcelona. It strikes me that with huge innocence and true generosity, Brad Pitt is building for the poor of New Orleans the kind of house that Brad Pitt would enjoy living in.

*

The pace of life in New Orleans is different. If I hadn't already known it, I think the taxi ride from the airport might have given me a clue.

It was twilight and there was no traffic to speak of, but it was the slowest cab ride I can ever recall taking. I watched the lights in the tall buildings of the Business District twinkling against the violet sky as we swung up onto the freeway, and braced myself for the usual surge of acceleration. But instead of putting his foot down the driver continued to cruise equably while he asked me where I was from, and reflected aloud on where my destination – Spruce Street – might be. 'On the River side of Claiborne? Uh-huh. Yes, I believe I know it. There's a whole neighbourhood of streets named after trees. Spruce, Maple, Birch. I think we'll be able to find it.'

An elderly white man with thick, round spectacle lenses that seemed to glow in the twilight with their own illumination, he drove equably and with care. We reached a district of tree-lined boulevards where big, ornate wooden houses resplendent with pillars and jutting upper storeys loomed up in the taxi's lights like ships and then vanished into darkness.

'We don't have North and South, or East and West in New Orleans', he explained. 'We have Riverside and Lakeside, and we have Uptown and Downtown. City's built in a curve of the Mississippi River, so it doesn't have a grid the way most American cities do. It's kind of like a bicycle wheel or a fan, with the streets radiating out like the spokes.'

This perspective once established, the scene was set for him to tell me his life history, and by the time we reached Spruce Street I could have compiled a pretty good *Who's Who* entry for him. I knew about his Greek father; I knew that his mother grew up as one of seven children on an east Louisiana farm. I knew where he'd taken his degree, and all about his first job as an industrial chemist, including how many weeks' annual holiday he got. I was also well-informed about his uncle, who invented a type of flame-proof cotton and spent much of his time travelling the world franchising the patent to manufacturers in different countries (we agreed that he must have visited my home town of Manchester, then England's leading textile centre).

There was much more, but even at twenty-nine miles per hour, and allowing a little time to consult a well-thumbed street index, Spruce Street couldn't be postponed forever. By the time it arrived, I'd learned something important about New Orleans: namely, that conversation, stories and people are generally more important there than time or money. We reached our destination, we both enjoyed the journey, and we got to know each other a little. If he ever gives me a ride again we'll have a lot of catching up to do. I never did discover how a retired industrial chemist came to be driving a cab, but maybe he does it for the company. And, as he hauled my bags from the trunk in front of 1473 Spruce Street, he uttered a prophecy.

'If you're spending time in New Orleans', he said, 'you won't get bored, and you won't go hungry.'

*

The voodoo priestess is called Ellie. She's petite, white, and wearing a floaty cotton dress with an embroidered yoke. We're in the coffee shop at the corner of Esplanade and Decatur, which is famous for its home-baked muffins. She tells me that what I call voodoo is properly 'vodou', and goes on to explain about the *lwa*. The word is pronounced, roughly, 'loo-*ah*', and it means the Vodou gods. Some of what she tells me is enough to put me off the muffin I'm eating but I carry on sipping my coffee.

'My own personal *lwa* is Maman Brigitte. She's Queen of the Dead, and she's married to Baron Samedi, lord of the cemetery. You can recognise her because her ears and nostrils are stuffed with cotton like those of a corpse.'

'How did you know she was your own *lwa*?' I ask. 'Did she communicate with you somehow?'

'No, Mama, our *mambo*, the priestess who taught us, told each of her pupils who their individual *lwa* would be. She works it out from seeing the kind of person you are, your temperament, your personality. Or you may just get possessed by that *lwa* at a ceremony. You see people suddenly taken over, their whole posture changes, the shape of their body, and they can start talking in a different voice too. You can often recognise the *lwa* by the particular voice.' She looks thoughtful. 'Maman Brigitte doesn't talk, though, because she has a white cloth tied round her jaw to keep it shut.' She sips her coffee. 'Like a corpse, you know.'

I ponder this information. Maman Brigitte has a pretty name, but don't think I want to meet her.

'So were you initiated here in New Orleans?' I ask.

'I was taught here. But Mama took us to Haiti for the initiations. We went twice, and that was an ordeal in itself. Haiti's about the poorest country in the world. The poverty and dirt were unbelievable. We don't go any more because it got too dangerous. A couple of years ago Mama's teacher said he simply couldn't guarantee our safety any longer. So now he comes over here instead.

'It's an odd thing,' she says, 'but for the black people in New Orleans vodou is mostly superstitions and folklore. It's mainly the white people who follow it as an organised religion. And traditionally it's led by women. There've always been white or mixed-race vodou priestesses in New Orleans.'

There are several vodou temples in the city, as well as the many shops (known as *botanicas* because of the herbs they sell) where you can buy spells – magic powders, candles, good luck charms, images.

'I used to run a shop, a *botanica*, downtown, and I used to get a lot of respect from people on the street. I could see people looking at me as I passed and getting out of the way. And then they'd come in and ask for advice – about their job, about their marriage.'

'And could you help them?'

'There isn't much that a bit of common-sense advice and a house blessing can't fix. You should come and meet Mama.'

She rummages in her big embroidered cloth shoulder-bag, taking out a small pad and ballpoint pen. With great concentration, she begins drawing a careful diagram: two horizontal lines; two more vertical lines crossing them. Along one horizontal line she writes *DESIRE* and along the other *PIETY*. Between them she draws a small square with a cross inside it. Up one vertical line she writes the words *ST CLAUDE*. Underneath she draws a third horizontal line with many little crossbars like a zipper.

'That's the train track', she explains. 'Mama's shop is at 835 Piety Street. It's called The Island of Salvation Botanica. The temple's just behind, in Rosalie Alley, between Piety and Desire. Both streets run off St Claude just east of the French Quarter so it's easy to find.'

I take the map and we finish our coffee. Ellie's going to show me the tomb of Marie Laveaux, the nineteenth-century Voodoo Queen of New Orleans. We stroll along North Rampart Street away from the stuccoed blocks of the French Quarter with their iron balconies and wooden shutters, and into an industrial district with blocks of dusty-looking tenements between workshops and warehouses. We move through alternating blazes of heat and pools of shadow as we pass along under the live-oak trees lining the street, heavy-limbed giants that sprawl in the air, filling the sky with a green trembling shade. At a corner as we wait to cross I notice a mass of jasmine seething up a wooden telephone pole, starry with white flowers, loading the air with sweet, piercing perfume. Louisiana's luxuriant subtropical growth is flourishing even here.

A little way along the street is a small grey church with three arches along the front and a squat spire above. Ellie takes me down the side of the church. At the back is Basin Street, lined with a high white wall, blinding in the midday sun. A rusty iron gate in the wall opens onto strange terrain. It's a crowded miniature city of dazzling white oddly-shaped houses some six to eight feet high, jostling together at all angles, with tortuous paths zigzagging between as if threading a maze. A notice tells us that this is St Louis Cemetery No. 1, and that defacing the graves and monuments is strictly forbidden.

We set out along the path between the tombs. They're built like little houses for the dead because New Orleans soil is so waterlogged that burying bodies underground won't work. Most of the overground tombs are dedicated to entire families. Some are white marble, some are just whitewashed. The glare makes me wish I'd brought sunglasses.

We stop in front of a large white-painted tomb covered with graffiti. A marble plaque on one end announces in French that it's the burial place of the *Famille Laveaux*, and a plaque underneath specifies *Veuve Paris*, the Widow Paris. Ellie tells me that Marie Laveaux's married name was Paris, so the widow is the lady we're looking for.

'Anything people want,' says Ellie, 'they just ask her for it. And she can fix it. There's a whole special procedure. You have to put three crosses on the tomb.' Stepping carefully around the clutter of miscellaneous rubbish on the ground in front of the tomb, I take a closer look at the graffiti. Sure enough, the grubby white surface is covered with triple crosses, XXX, drawn in marker pen, pencil, wax crayon, lipstick, eyeliner… whatever the petitioner had on them at the time, I suppose.

'Okay,' says Ellie, 'so after you draw your crosses, you knock three times on the tomb to call Marie. And you ask her for what you want. Then you turn around three times clockwise. And you leave an offering.' So that explains the mass of trash on the stone paving. There's a chaos of things. Coins and bunches of withered flowers are strewn everywhere. There are also silk flowers, strings of Mardi Gras beads (purple, green and gold), a playing card (Jack of Diamonds), bottles of scent, burnt-down candles, sweets in twists of paper. There's a red-and-buff plastic asthma inhaler. A teddy bear. A bottle of what looks like rum, though a closer look identifies it as iced tea. Someone has left their Safeway storecard as a gift for Marie. There's a fat, faded paperback copy of *Atlas Shrugged* by Ayn Rand. I lift the cover gingerly and find a stamp saying *Warren Easton Senior High School*. I wonder what teenage trauma that book commemorates. I hope Marie made things better.

I'm not going to wake Marie up and ask her favours: I don't think I need anything that badly right now. But before we leave I scrabble in my pocket and drop a couple of coins into a small wicker basket at the centre of the mess. For what they're worth.

'Now I'm going to show you something really strange', says Ellie. 'Something for emergencies.'

We cross the road again to the little grey church. Opening the door under the central arch, we step into the cool, silent interior. It has a sharp, pungent waxy smell with a tinge of lavender. I can see a statue of Our Lady of Guadalupe standing in an elongated gold sunburst over the altar, but Ellie steers me round to the right, pointing up at the wall beside the door. High on a stone bracket stands an almost life-size statue, fully coloured, of a young man with curly dark hair dressed like a Roman soldier. He holds out a small wooden cross with *Hodie* written on it and seems to be crushing a bird under his foot. On the bracket that supports him is the word EXPEDITE.

'That's St Expedite', says Ellie. 'He's a real New Orleans saint, he doesn't seem to exist anywhere else. The story they tell is that he came to New Orleans some time in the nineteenth century when they ordered a whole batch of Catholic saints for a church, I don't know where from, I guess maybe Italy or Spain. Anyway the saints had labels on but this one had lost its label. But it had a sticker on the outside from the shipping company saying *Expedite* so they thought his name must be St Expedite, and here he is. I don't know if it's true.

'The point is, he's the saint you call on if you need something really fast. Like, *right now*. He's supposed to deliver instantly.'

Young St Expedite certainly seems full of vigour, rosy-cheeked and curly-haired, thrusting his little wooden cross forward. It seems a paradox that this instant-delivery saint, who might be a patron for the modern world with its hurry and impatience, should be popular in laid back New Orleans. But then, maybe that's exactly why he's needed: to deliver the instant fix, after you've left everything too late for too long.

We leave the church and I say goodbye to Ellie. I still have her hand-drawn map, and I promise I'll come and meet her Mama one day soon, in that temple hidden away somewhere between Piety and Desire.

*

We're two blocks from the French Quarter, walking down Frenchmen street and looking for music. Not that it's hard to find. Every other doorway on Frenchmen is a club or a bar and music's coming out of them all. I can hear rap pumping from a black doorway with purple light inside and a group of guys holding beer bottles hanging out on the step. Next door, a place that was once a shop has its plateglass window painted over in a wash of psychedelic colours and plastered with posters advertising music, theatre and burlesque shows. A heavy metal rock band's playing inside. We stop at a bar whose doors and windows are wide open to the night air. A long wooden sign across the front of the building reads, in hand painted letters, *The Spotted Cat.* People are milling slowly around, drifting in and out, holding glasses. There's a jazz quartet playing, and about a foot inside the door, a young guy with a bandana tightly bound over his dreadlocks is playing a tenor sax above a driving rhythm section. It's some of the most intricate and accomplished modern jazz I've ever heard: Charlie Parker-style music, an endless torrent of rippling notes floating and butterflying all over the place, dipping in and out of discords, clashing and then making up, touching on the underlying chord pattern just often enough so that you know he hasn't lost his bearings completely. His cheeks shiny and inflated, he doesn't ever seem to pause for breath until with a final exuberant rush of notes he breaks off to an explosion of applause and lets the pianist take over. He wipes his mouth and reaches for a glass perched on the windowsill beside him.

'In New York you'd pay a fortune to listen to music like this', Ken murmurs. We manoeuvre ourselves into the bar and find seats: a dilapidated office chair for me, and the end of a sofa with seriously broken springs into which Ken sinks until it's a question whether he'll ever be able to get out again. The oddly-assorted tables are stained and sticky, the floor is bare and splintered boards. While the piano solo continues, I get off my chair and wedge myself into the crowd at the bar. I wait for service, waving a ten-dollar bill for attention. The back of the bar is a long, long mirror with an army of bottles ranked in front of it on a shelf. In the middle of the shelf stands a wooden statue of a white cat with black spots. Its hugely elongated neck reaches nearly to the ceiling, a little round head perched on top. The Spotted Cat! I secure a couple of Budweisers and make my way back.

The pianist finishes his riff, rolls off his stool and heads for the bar, leaving the drummer and bassist to solo. Near the bar the pianist engages in some negotiations with another man, who slaps him on the back, wanders across to the band, settles himself on the piano stool and, after a few abrupt experimental chords here and there, Thelonius Monk style, melds into the ensemble while the saxophonist wipes the mouthpiece of his instrument on a cloth from his pocket, tongues the reed a bit, and resumes playing.

A very young white man (he looks scarcely eighteen), with a rucksack on his back, hangs about timidly near the door. I guess he's a tourist, probably a jazz fan from up north or from Europe, come to see if New Orleans is really all that he's heard. When the quartet has finished another number and embarked on a third, I notice the tenor player, in full flow, gesturing at the youth with the bell of his sax, and making significant eye-rolling expressions. The young guy steps inside the bar and unshoulders the rucksack. Opening it, he takes out an alto sax. About five bars later, he and the tenor man are playing duets. The tenor breaks off to give the young altoist a solo – he's good, but not on the level of the tenorist, though he gets plenty of applause – and they wind up playing alternate eight-bar breaks to the end of the number.

So much for my notion that he was a tourist. On a table by the pianist's elbow is a pint glass, and curled inside it a piece of paper with the handwritten word *TIPS*. We both put money in it when we leave. For all I know, the contents of that glass may be the only payment these guys will get tonight.

*

'Not that it's at all likely,' says Ken, 'but if you should hear gunfire, just hit the ground as fast as you can.'

It's lunchtime the next day, and we've driven out to North Claiborne Avenue in the Tremé, one of New Orleans's oldest working-class districts, to follow the street parade of the Old & Nu Style Fellas Social Aid and Pleasure Club. We're hoping to be part of the 'second line' – the motley collection of passers-by and people with nothing better to do that tags on to the back of any New Orleans street parade, following the 'first line' – the band itself.

New Orleans has a big array of 'Social Aid and Pleasure Clubs': organisations that began in the nineteenth century to provide insurance for African Americans, who weren't served by the big insurance companies. Naturally they developed a festive dimension, and now every Sunday from January through midsummer there's a street parade somewhere in the city by one of the Clubs. Anyone who sees a street parade tends to stop whatever they're doing and follow it. They might as well, because the traffic will be held up and nothing much will get done until it's left the neighbourhood. The Clubs issue fliers setting out their planned routes, and we've noticed that this one's passing near us so we might as well join it.

We park the car on the 'neutral ground' (New Orleansspeak for the central reservation) under the concrete overpass that runs the full length of North Claiborne carrying Interstate 10. The Avenue used to be a fine boulevard shaded by live-oak trees, and people used to socialise and sit out on the neutral ground under the trees, but in the 1960s a 'coloured' neighbourhood was regarded as expendable and the powers of the city in their wisdom decided to run the interstate highway right down the middle, felling the live-oaks and replacing them with the concrete piers of the freeway, which now march all the way along the centre of the avenue, bringing a perpetual thunder of traffic. The neutral ground is a dusty wilderness. Local artists have tried to brighten it up by painting vivid murals on some of the concrete pillars: landscapes, local heroes, flags, groups of children. It's brave, but it doesn't make up for the lost trees.

So we park in the hot shadow of the Interstate and Ken takes everything moveable out of the car interior and locks it in the boot, admitting that this is a dangerous neighbourhood. People are milling about: guys in t-shirts and jeans, women with parasols shepherding small children in smart shirts and bowties or puffy cotton dresses and tight pigtails. Teenagers sit on the bonnets of cars drinking from beer cans. Someone messes about with the squawk button on a loud hailer. There's no sign of the parade so we buy an Abita Amber and a hotdog each from a vendor's cart and wait.

After a few minutes the crowd starts pulling itself together spontaneously, moving out from under the shadow of the Interstate into the burning sun. People are pointing up the Avenue, and sure enough, the parade is coming. The first thing I can hear is the thud of a bass drum. Other percussion sorts itself out from the distant blur of sound and at the same time I can make out figures approaching down the Avenue: white shirts, pale blue umbrellas, silver and brass instruments. There's an open-topped car at the front, and perched up on swathes of peach-coloured satin on the back of it a lady who looks like a black version of the Queen, the English Queen, in a pale blue dress and hat, holding a huge fan of pale blue ostrich plumes and waving to the crowd. Then come the musicians: trombones and trumpets leading, tubas close behind puffing out the bass notes. Bass drums and side drums behind them, providing a bouncy, syncopated rhythm for the repetitious, almost military phrase the brass instruments are playing over and over again. A woman in pale blue wheels a pushchair with a small toddler alongside the band. The musicians are followed by a group of men in white shirts, white hats and grey trousers with braces. They hold white handkerchiefs like morris dancers and they tapdance their way along on the scorching concrete of the road surface. The street's lined with spectators who are kept back by men holding a blue nylon rope taut as they walk alongside the parade, but everyone surges in afterwards, and we're carried with them until we're half walking, half dancing our way up the street in the middle of a huge crowd carrying plastic cups of beer, wheeling prams, leading children, taking photos, and eating chicken out of cardboard cartons from Popeye's.

We cover several streets this way, turning off Claiborne onto Esplanade, North Rampart, and then Basin Street. When we finally break away and walk back to the car, nothing's been stolen or disturbed. The concrete piers recede into the distance, dusty gray and howling with unseen traffic. I notice that here and there, with sad irony, the piers of the freeway have been painted to look like big green oak trees.

*

It's almost a year to the next Mardi Gras, and Jazz Fest is still six weeks off, but restless New Orleans has to keep its spirits up, and this weekend it's French Quarter Fest. I ride the St Charles streetcar down to the waterfront. It's an old-fashioned tram, red and cream, with rounded ends and a big circular headlamp in the middle of the front exactly like the ones I remember from my childhood in Liverpool. People sit on creaky, varnished wooden seats gossiping and clutching their shopping bags. Somehow it doesn't feel like being in the USA: there's something European about it, and something old-fashioned English too. But then that applies to a lot of things in New Orleans.

When we reach the tram terminus I head down to the river behind a couple of bickering, elderly white tourists. 'I don't want to hear anything more that doesn't mean anything', the man is saying loudly. 'From now on, everything has to mean things.' I cross the street to the Mississippi riverfront and walk along to Audubon Park where most of the music will be.

It's already noon and I'm hungry so at the edge of the park I queue by a stall to get something to eat. I hesitate between two New Orleans specialities: a muffuletta and a po'boy. A muffuletta is a bread muffin about the size of my head, split in two and filled with layers of – starting from the bottom – chopped olive salad; Italian cheese; Swiss cheese; mortadella; salami; and sliced ham. You can have it hot or cold. A po'boy, on the other hand, is a foot-long, crisp baguette-type roll filled with wafer-thin sliced roast meat. In this case they're offering pork. New Orleans folklore has it that the po'boy is what poor boys used to eat. If so, they must have lived like kings. Any self-respecting New Orleans takeaway will bake its own bread, so the outside of the supercharged sandwich is usually as good as the filling. I decide a po'boy will be easier to eat and take one away.

The lawns between the walkway and the grey, sluggish Mississippi have stages erected every few hundred yards and the grass is crowded with people sitting on rugs, folding chairs or just the ground, listening to the music. I pass a stage with a 'brass band', which in New Orleans means a jazz band infinitely funkier, earthier and more musically adventurous than anything that goes by the name of 'traditional jazz' back in England. Another stage has a Gospel choir. Further on I stop to listen to a man who looks like Gene Vincent in a cowboy hat tell us it's time for 'Louisiana's national anthem' and lead the band into 'Jambalaya'.

I sit on the edge of a stone terrace above the river walk to eat my po'boy and watch, with surprise, an old-fashioned Mississippi riverboat moving out into the channel, paddle wheel churning at the rear, slender twin smokestacks fuming.

I'm not the only one who's eating. To my left perches a big lady in the yellow t-shirt that marks her as a festival security guard. She's tucking into chicken and rice from a styrofoam container. Having finished it she produces another box, this time full of brownies, and starts on that.

She catches my eye and smiles. 'You visiting here?'

'Yes ma'am', I say, emulating New Orleans formality. 'I'm from England.'

After the usual exclamations, she asks if I'm enjoying my time in the French Quarter.

'I certainly am', I tell her. 'But I've seen more of the city than that. I have a friend who lives here and he's taken me out into the Ninth Ward and shown me some of the damage that's left after Katrina.'

The lady puts down her brownie carton. 'I don't know what they told you,' she says, 'but Katrina ain't the half of it. People blame Katrina, Katrina this, Katrina that, but it wasn't the hurricane done the damage. You know they blew up the levees on purpose?'

'Blew them up?' Startled, I lower my po'boy. 'Who did?'

'The Bush government. Those levees was blown up with dynamite, maybe some other kind of high explosive. Now, my aunt, she lived in the Lower Ninth and she was flooded out, but it wasn't the hurricane did it. It happened after the hurricane had gone. She heard the explosion. Katrina had gone over and everything was quiet and then there was this great *boom!* And a wall of water came pouring in like a tsunami. That wasn't no accident.'

'So why did they do that?'

'They wanted to clear the Ninth Ward, clear out the poor people. Only they did their calculations wrong and it flooded some rich people's areas too. You'll see the French Quarter, the places the rich people and the tourists go weren't flooded. They wanted to keep those, because those are the places that make money.'

A tall, wiry man with a short, grizzled beard and a black confederate-style cap, also wearing a yellow security-guard t-shirt, strolls up behind us and the lady introduces her husband, Leonard.

'I been telling him about what really happened with Katrina', she explains.

'Yes sir, Katrina was just the excuse. People outside New Orleans have no idea how it really was. You know there was people tried to get across the Mississippi Bridge over there to escape the water and the police fired on them? There was four teenagers killed. Police tried to say it was the army done it; but it was the prejudiced police.

'Then there was the helicopters. They sent helicopters that were supposed to rescue people but they didn't, and they said people on the roofs with rifles was shooting at them. But those people was firing into the air to attract attention because they wanted to be rescued. You think a guy stuck on his roof with water coming up all around is going to shoot at a helicopter? They was desperate to be taken off!'

'And then', his wife joins in, 'there's the question about those body bags. They say officially there was three thousand five hundred people killed. But the coroner's office asked for thirty thousand body bags. Now, who were they all for? And where are they now? We don't know. Nobody knows. But there's a lot of people still missing and nobody knows what happened to them. A *lot* of people.'

'So it was hushed up?'

'It was hushed up. A whole lot of things was hushed up. But it was all planned. We know about someone who was at a meeting with the police, and he had a call on his cell phone saying he needed to get his family out of the way right then, because the levees was going to be blown up. So he left the meeting right then and he got them out. So it was all planned before. Katrina was just the excuse. When you go home, you tell people that.'

Acknowledgements

I am grateful to the editors of the following periodicals, where some of these poems were first published: *The Christian Parapsychologist*, *The Interpreter's House*, *The London Magazine*, *The Manhattan Review*, *New Walk*, *PN Review*, *Poetry Folio 68* (Kent and Sussex Poetry Society), *Poetry London*, *Stand*, *Temenos Academy Review*, *The Times Literary Supplement*, and *The Warwick Review*.

'The Key' first appeared in the journal *Amnios* (Havana, Cuba) in a Spanish translation by Katherine M. Hedeen and Victor Rodriguez Nuñez. Part of 'Bed' was included in *Travels on the Dance Floor* (André Deutsch, 2008). 'Luna Park' and 'Fortune' were broadcast on KUSP Central Coast Public Radio, Santa Cruz, CA in 2011.

'The Apple Pip' appeared in the anthology *99 Words*, edited by Liz Gray (Darton, Longman and Todd, 2011). 'Browside' appeared in the anthology *Home* (Clan-U Press, 2007). 'Fortune' appeared in the anthology *Therefore I Am* (Clan-U Press, 2008). 'The Maldon Hawk' appeared in the anthology *Initiate*, edited by Jane Draycott (Blackwell, 2010). 'For Our Lady of Guadalupe' and 'Silver' III appeared in the anthology *Waiting on the Word: a poem a day in Advent*, edited by Malcolm Guite (Canterbury Press, 2015).

'The Letters' won the 2009 Stafford Poetry Prize. 'Cigar' won second prize in the 2014 Kent and Sussex Poetry Competition.

Shugborough Eclogues was commissioned by Staffordshire Library and Information Service and Stafford and District Arts Council. Special thanks to Andrew Baker, who proposed the commission.

I am also deeply grateful to Ken McCarthy, whose hospitality in New Orleans made possible the writing of 'Hurricane Music'; and to Professor John Kelly and the President and Fellows of St John's College, Oxford, where 'Oxford, Again', 'Stones' and some other poems were written during a sojourn as an Invited Visiting Scholar. I hope they will forgive me for spending time on poetry when I should have been doing more scholarly things.

I must also honour three departed friends: Peter Moorhouse, at whose home in the Duddon Valley 'Browside', 'Cosmos' and some other poems were written; Alan Ward, my tutor in Old English, without whose long-ago patience 'The Maldon Hawk' could not have been written; and Glyn Davies, who during his last illness heard and approved 'Cosmos'.

GL
September 2015